I0485591

The World Of Love

The Mandala Coloring book

By

S.B. Nozaz

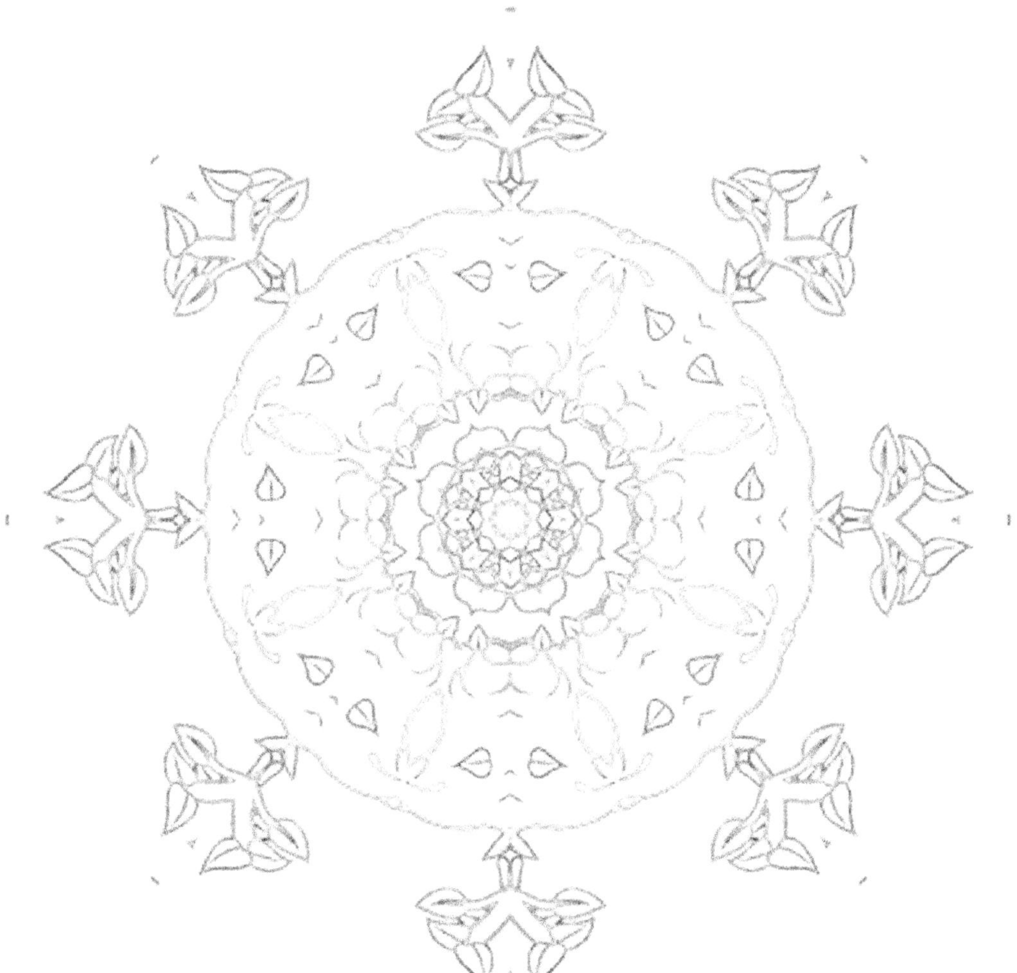

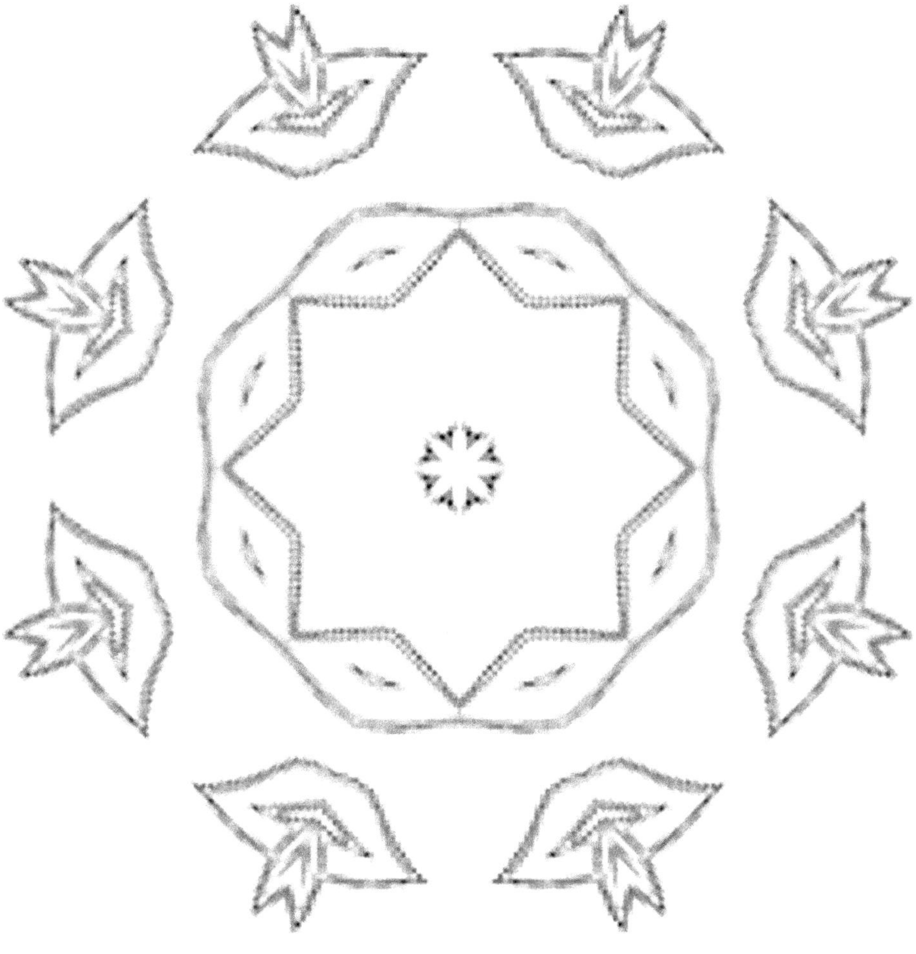

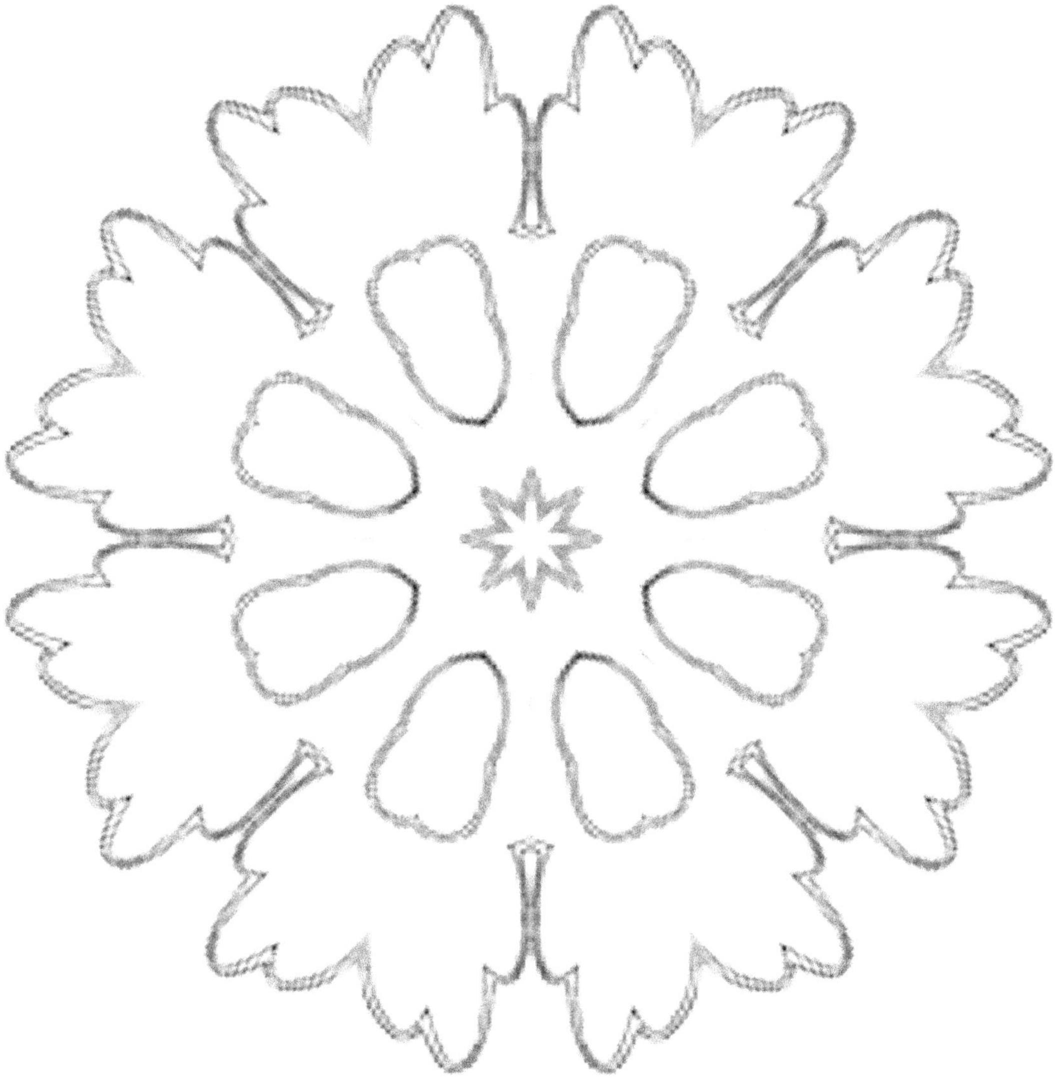

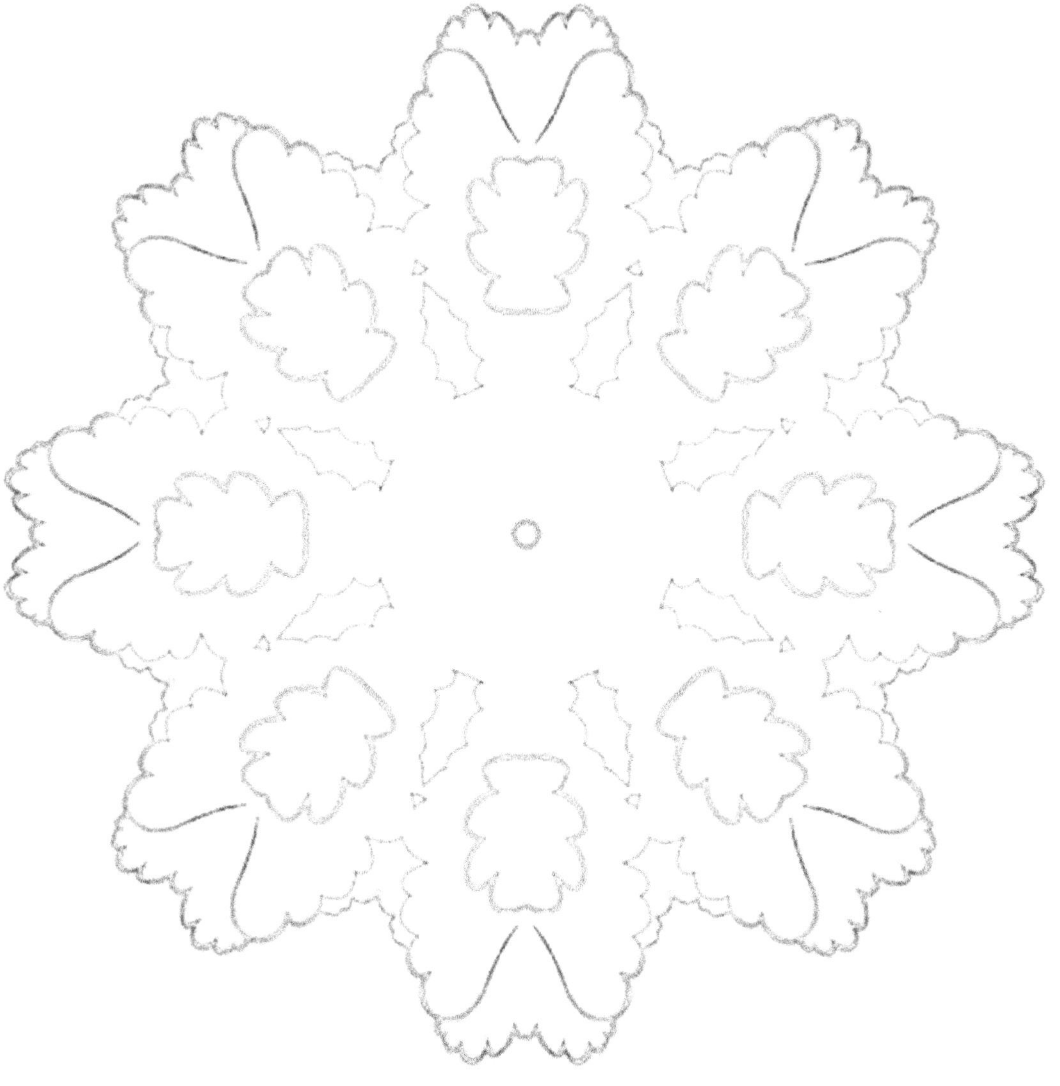

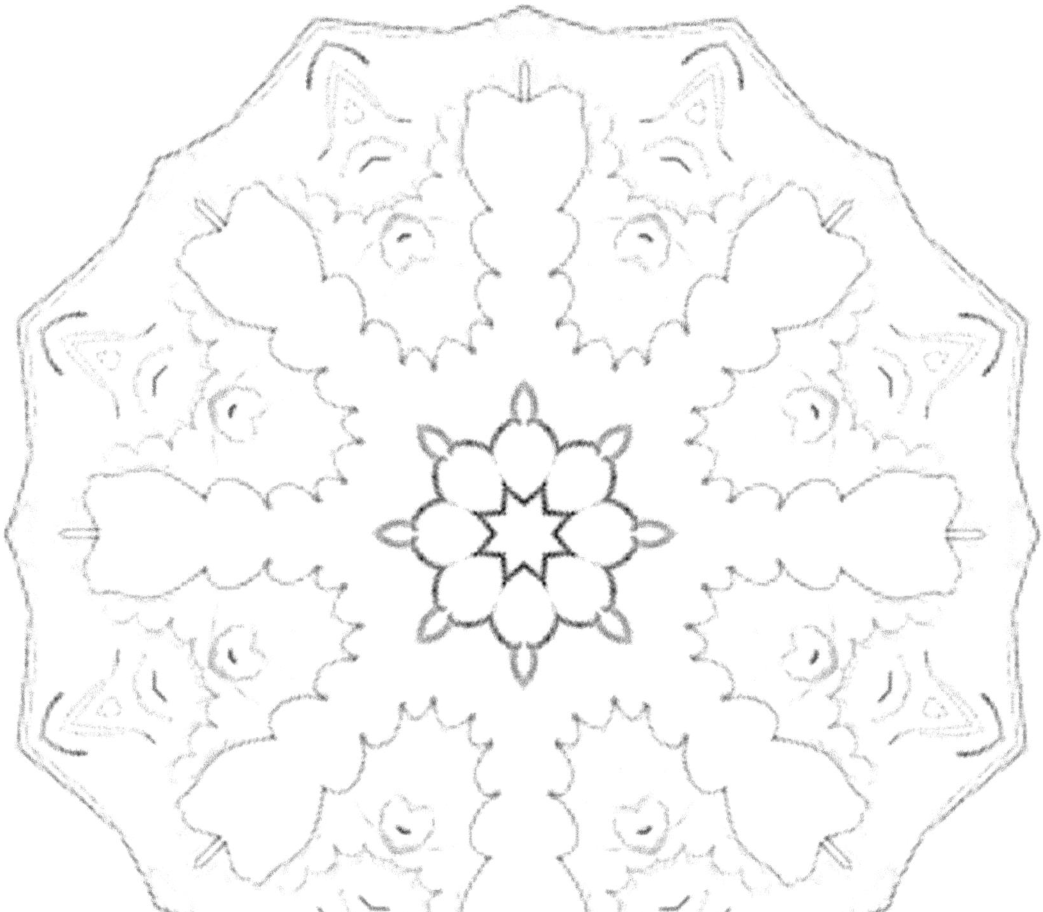

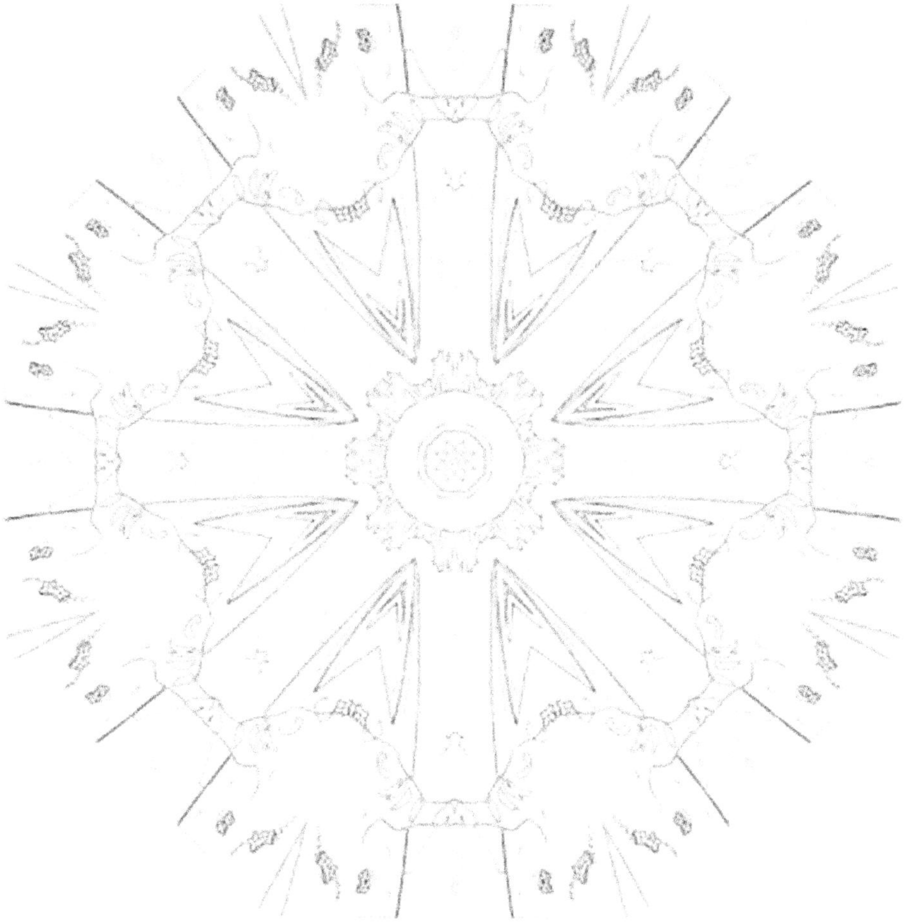

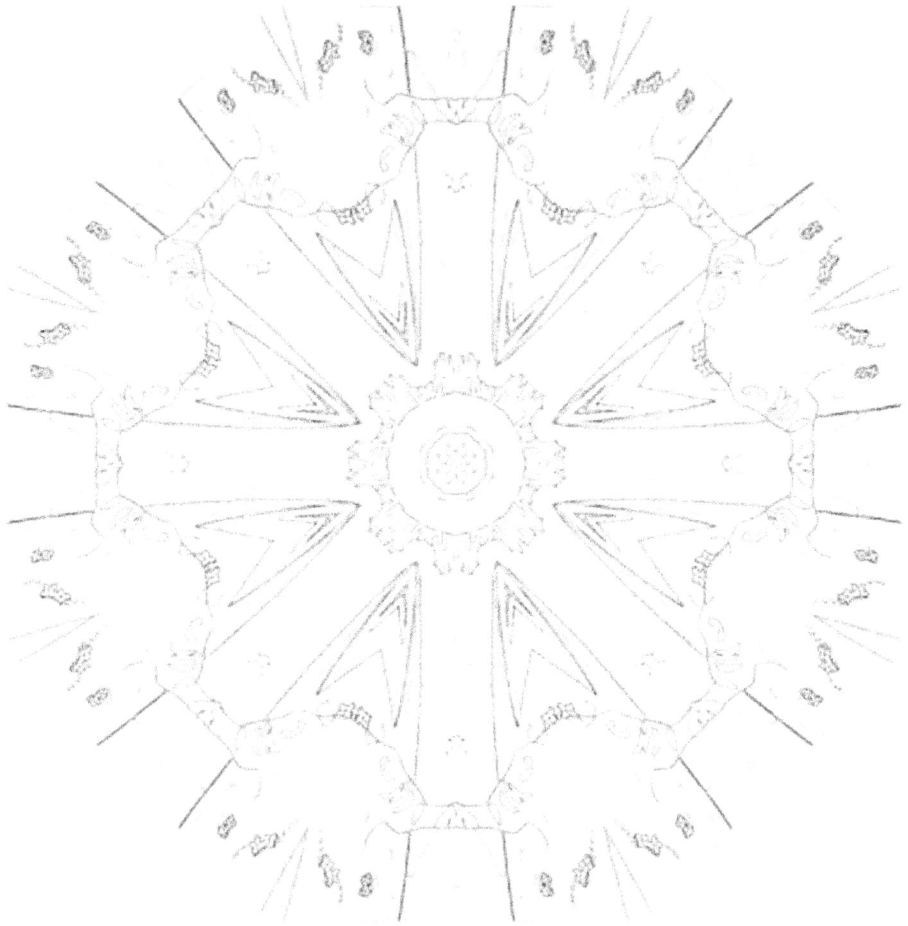

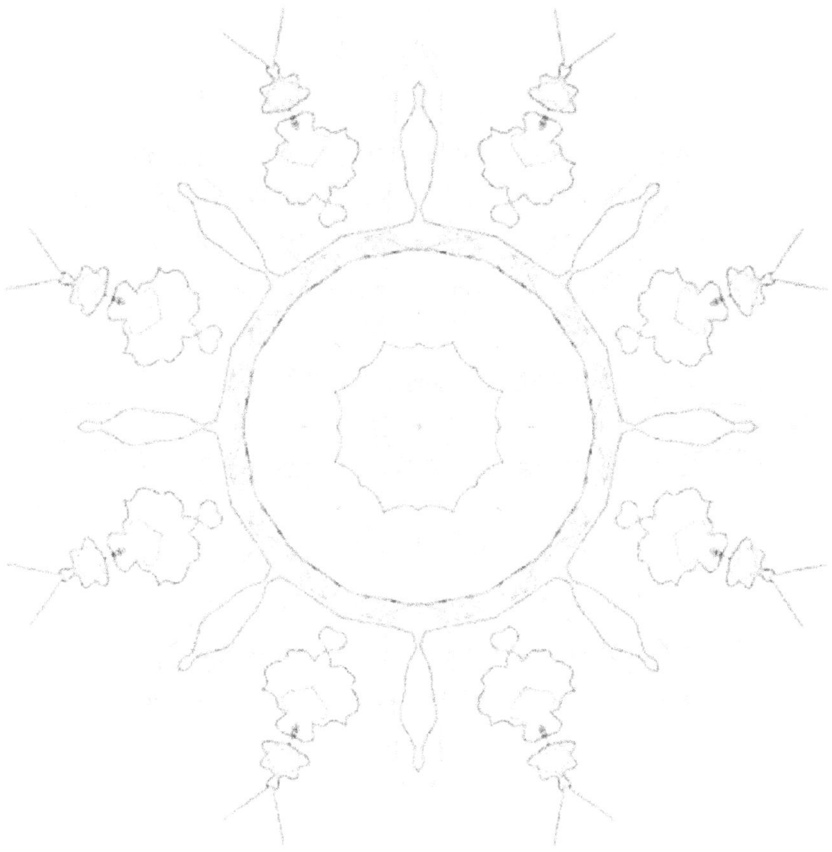

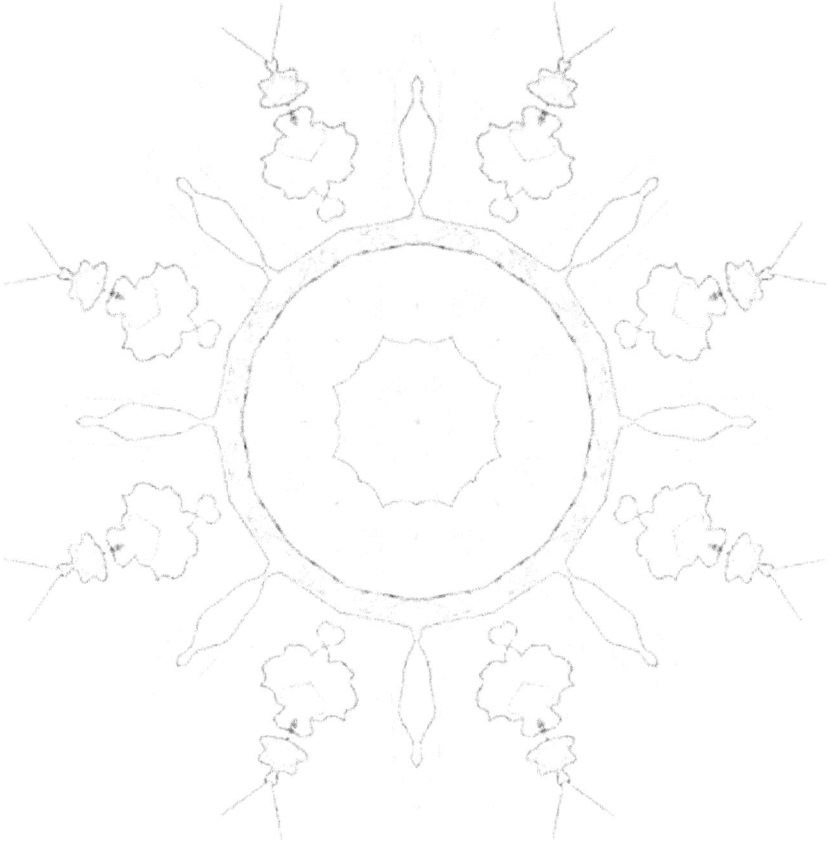

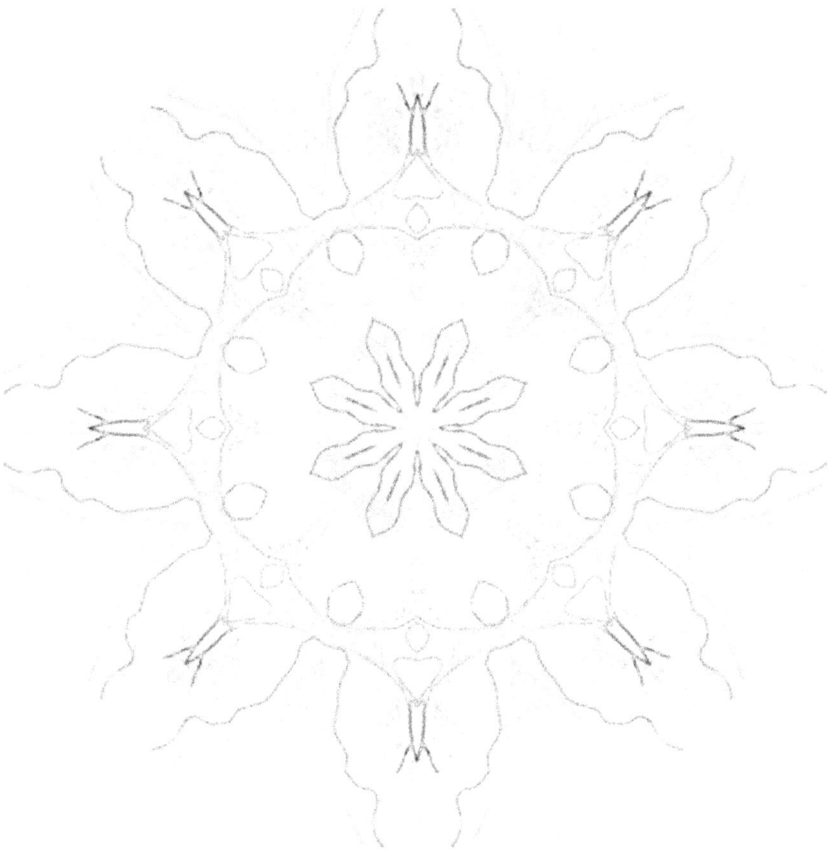

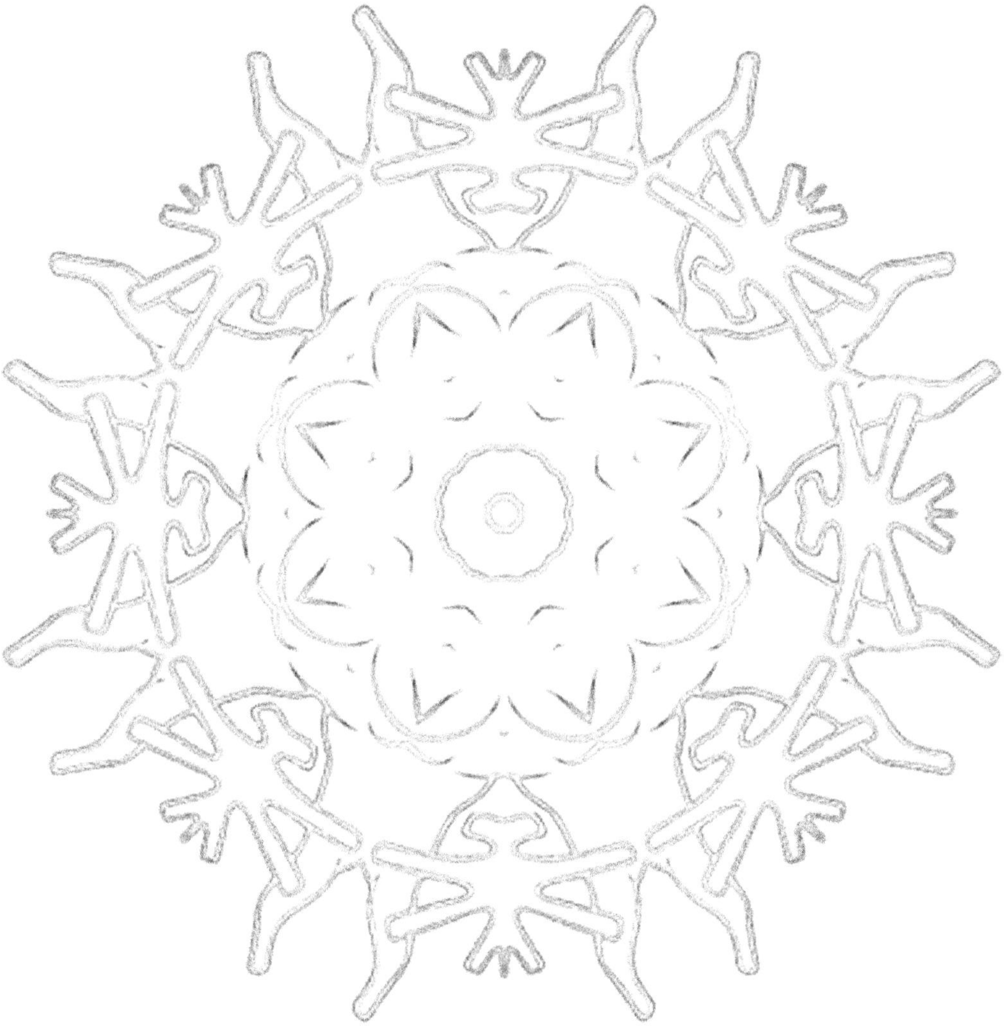

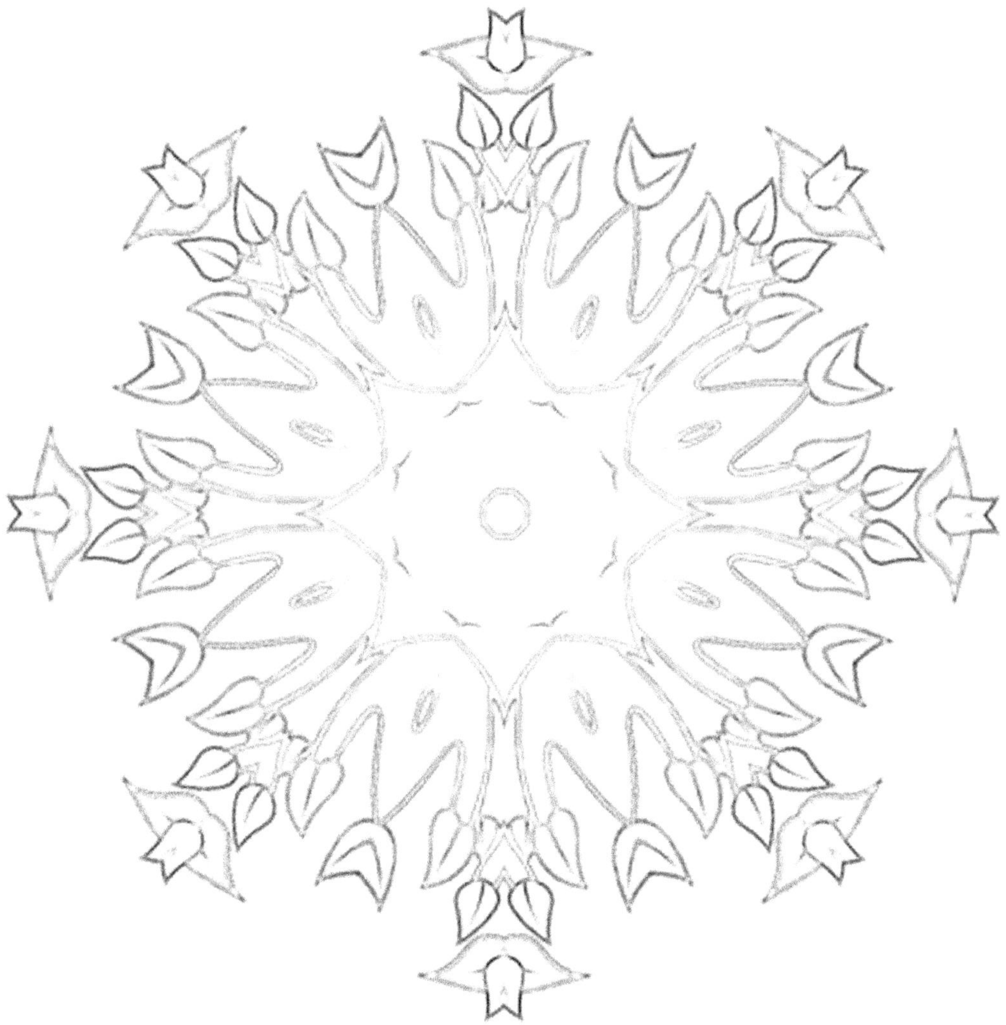

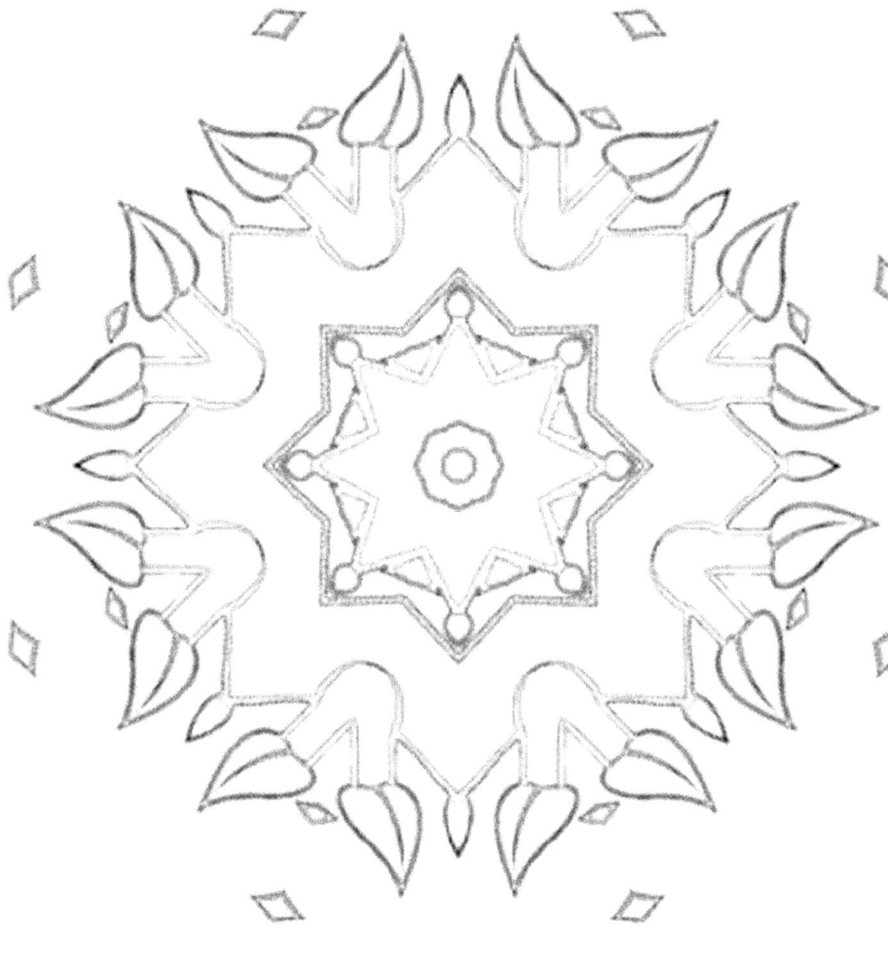

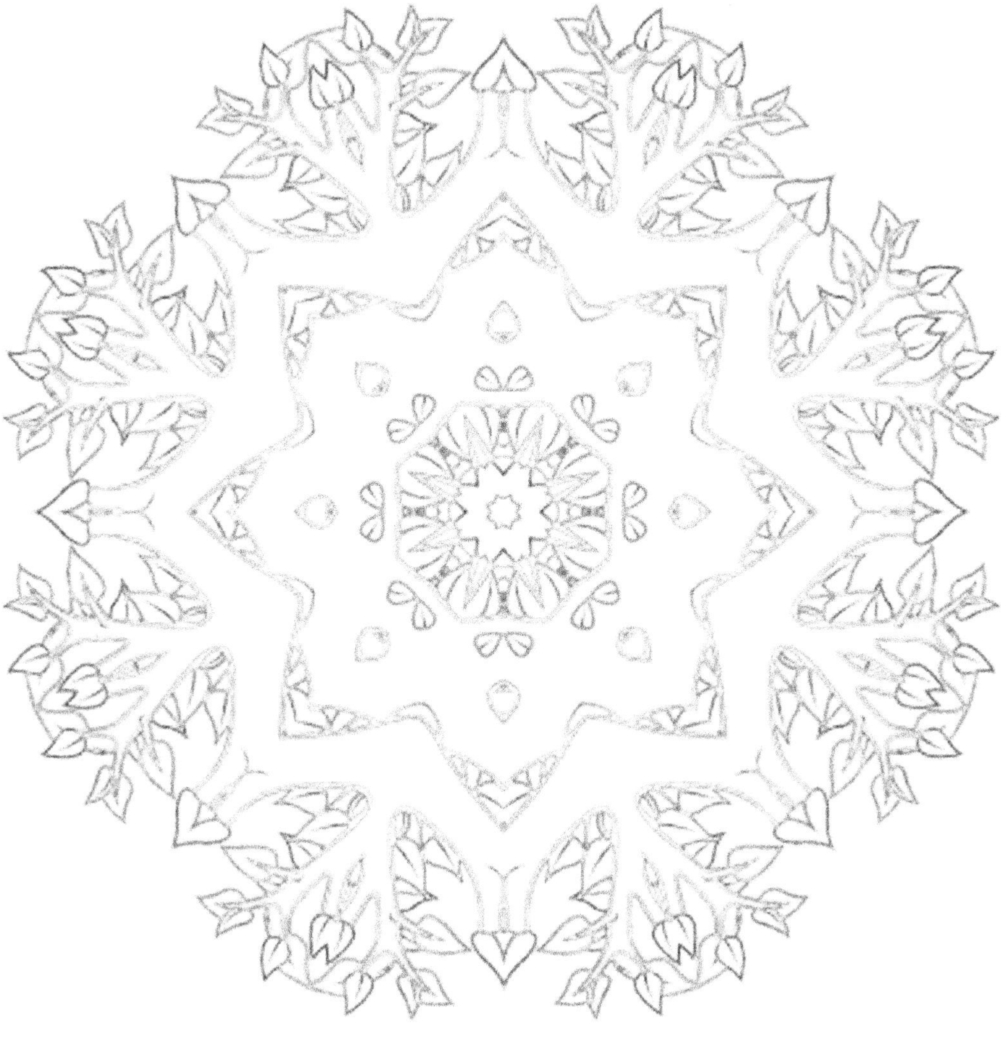

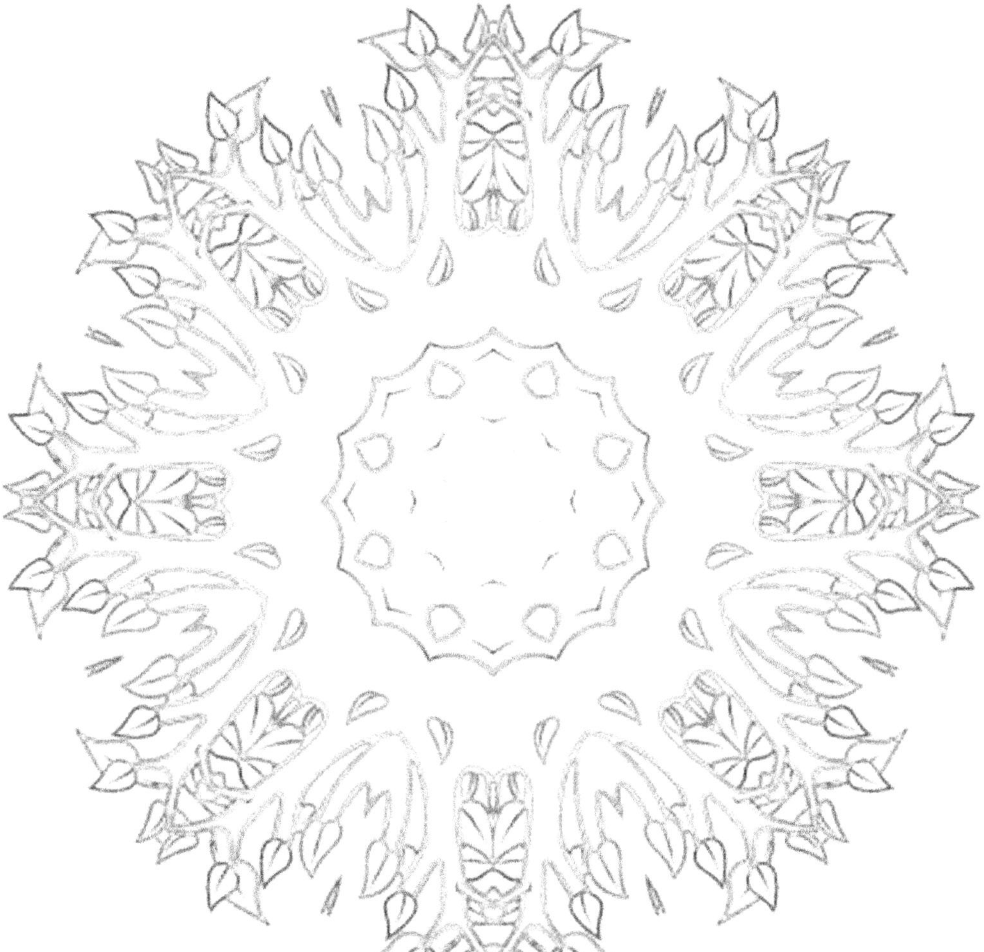

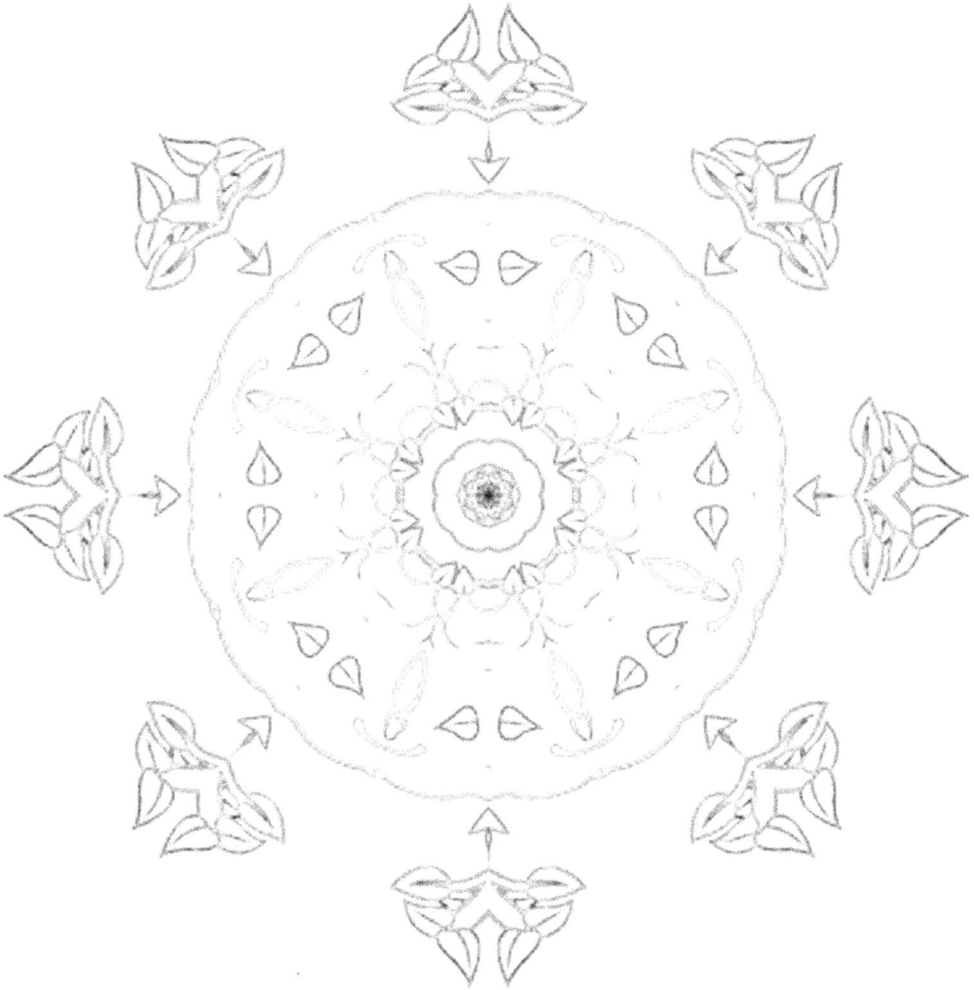

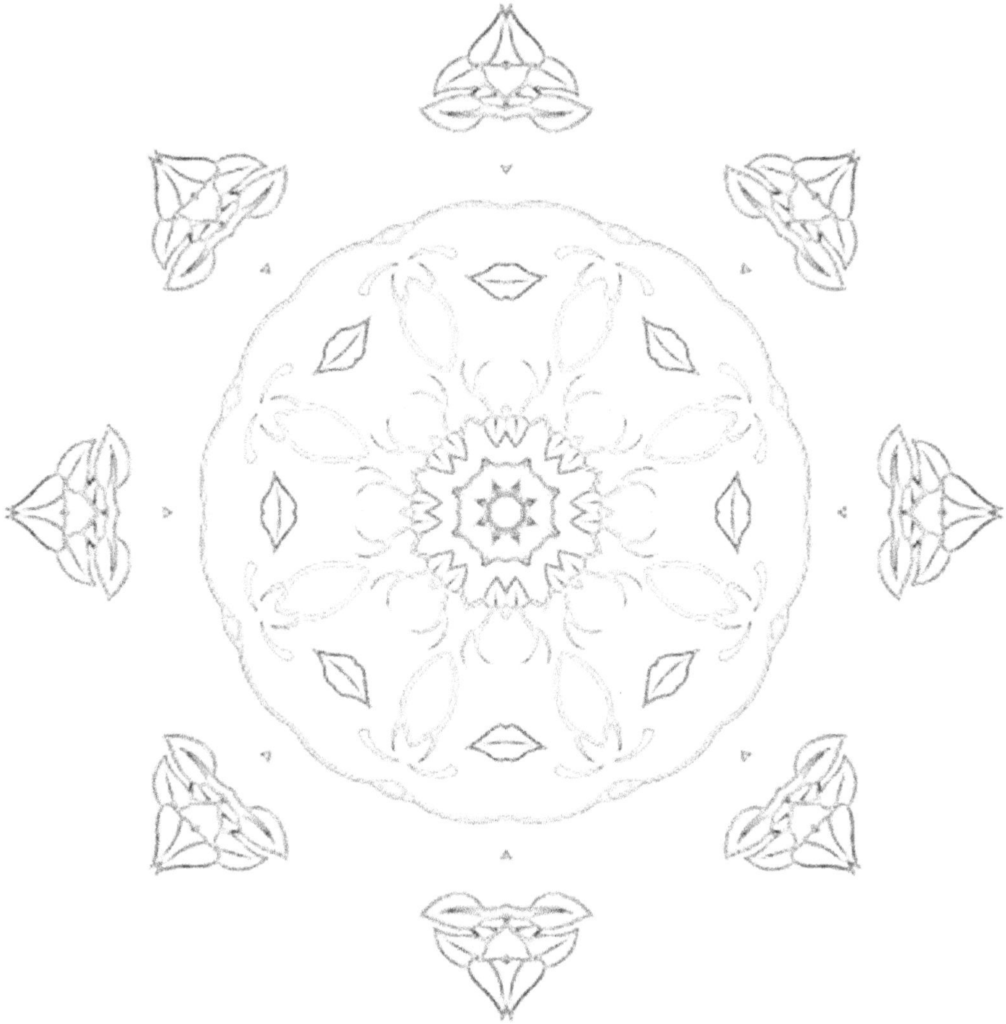

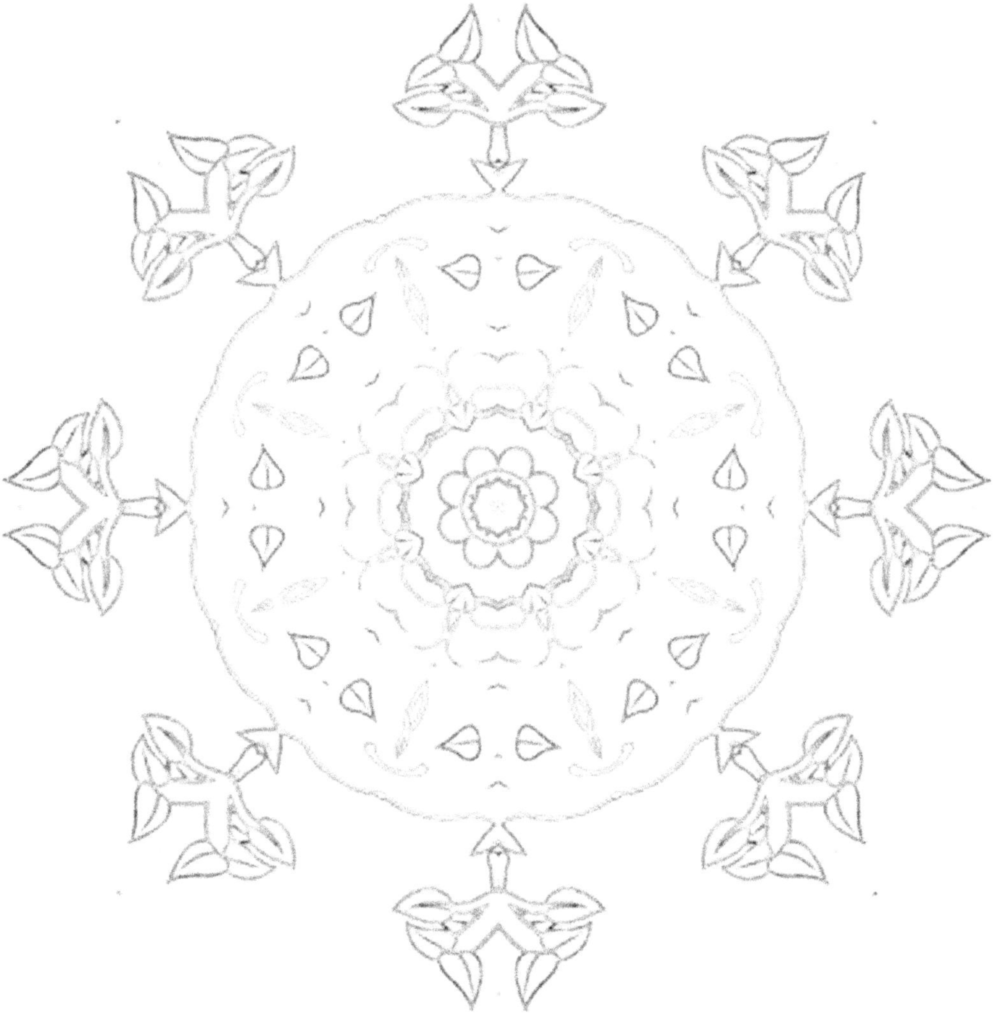

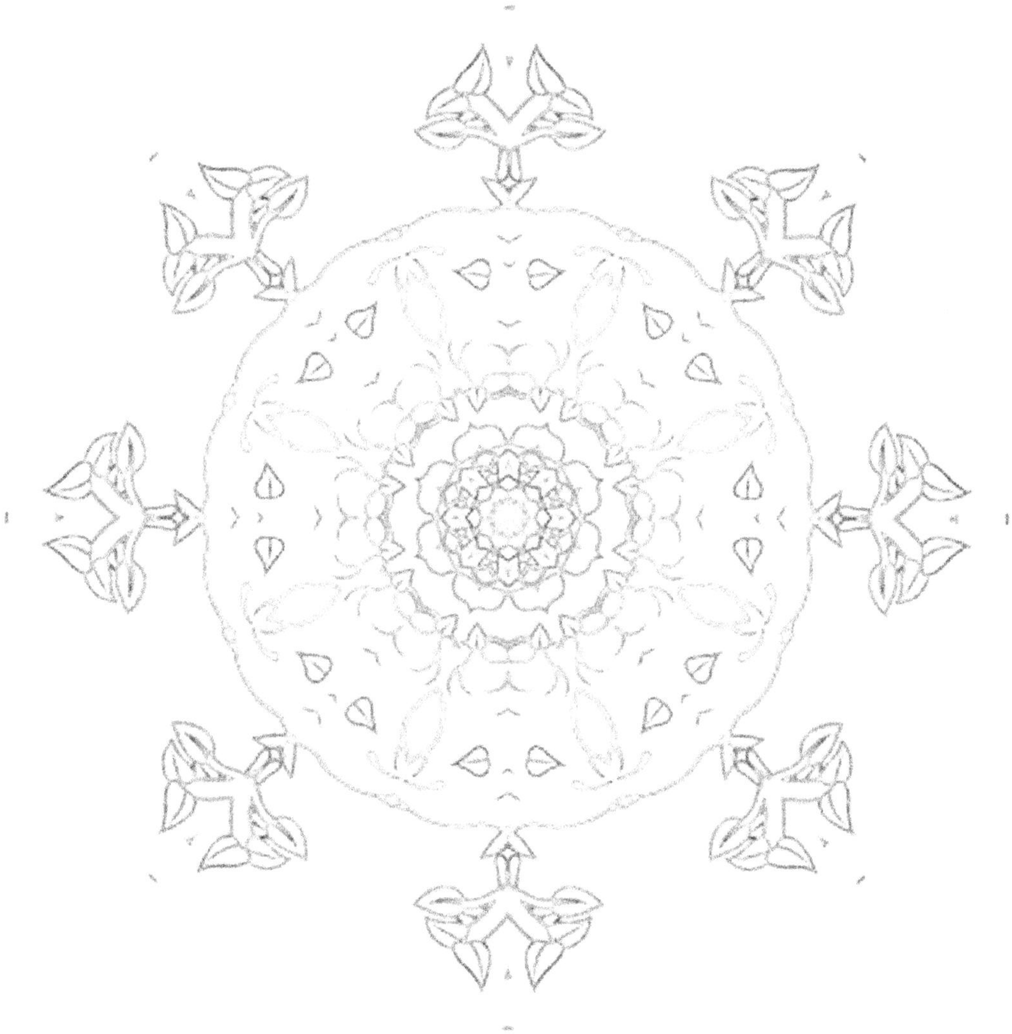

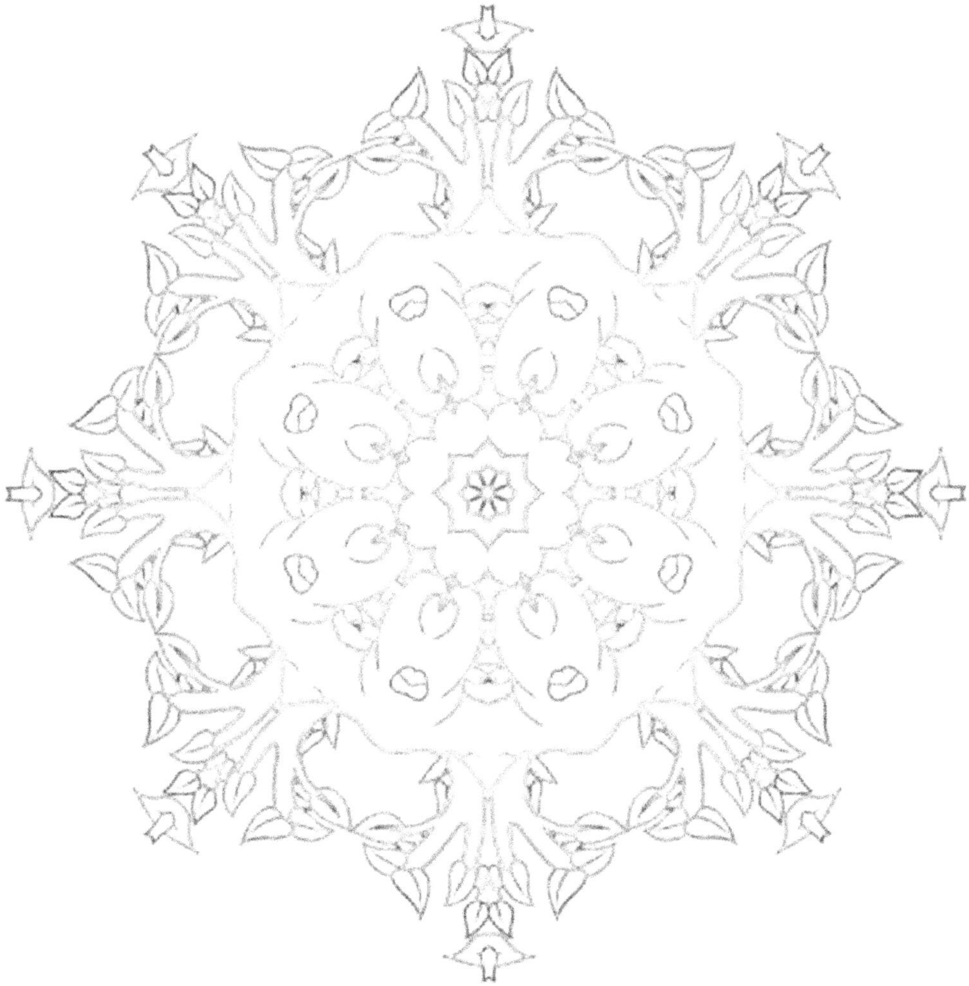

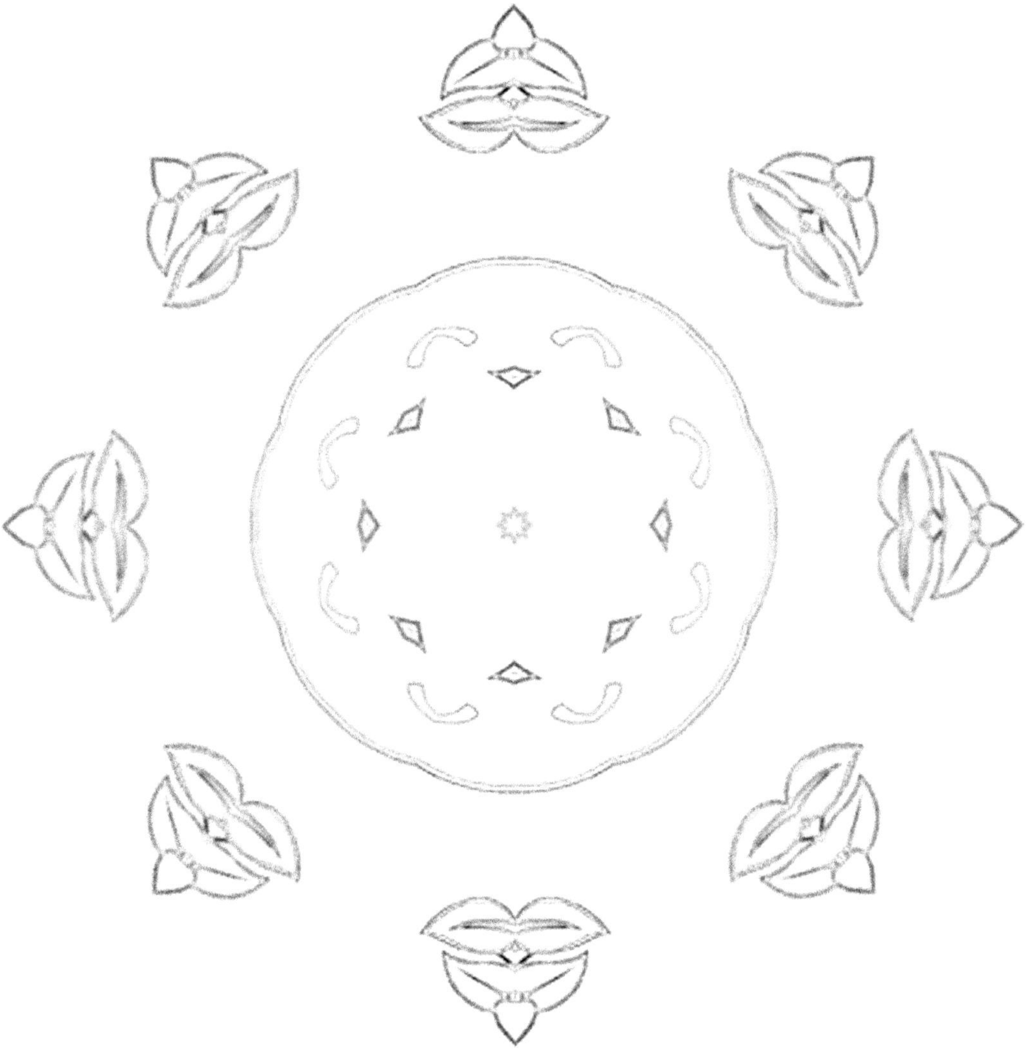

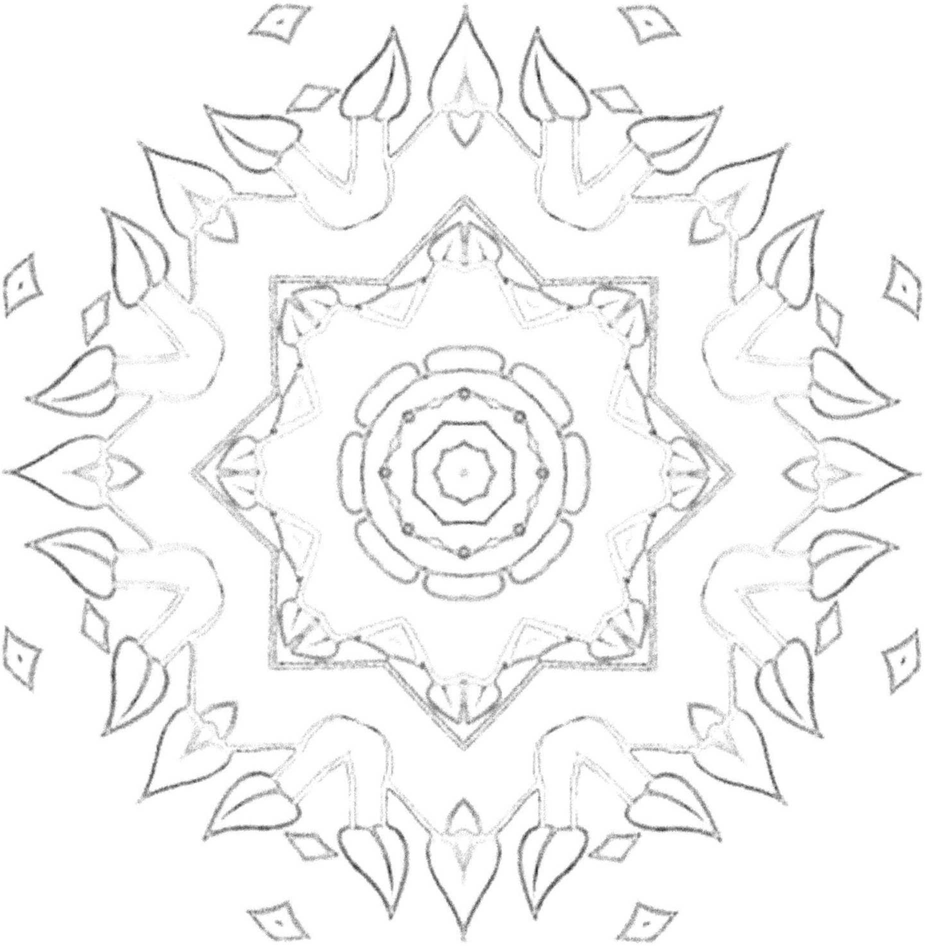

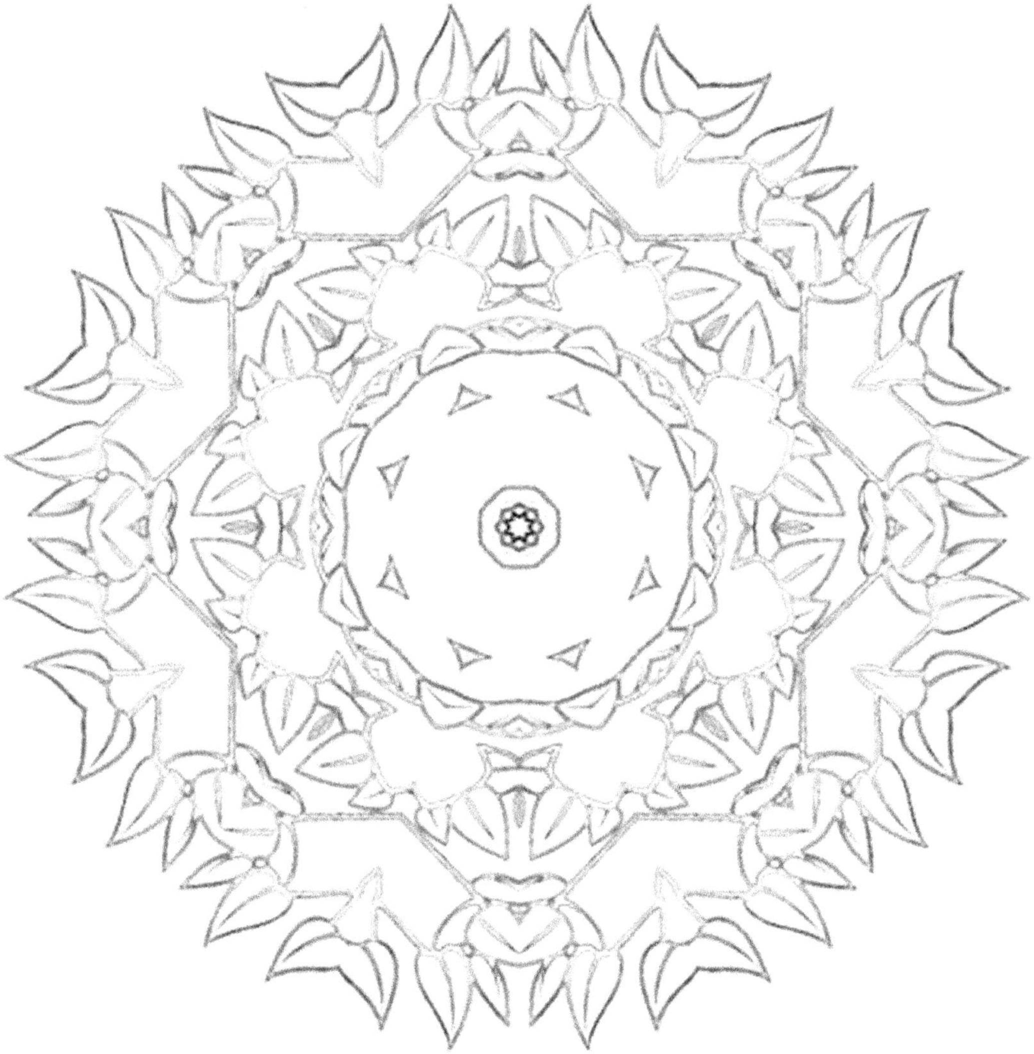

Note

www.ingramcontent.com/pod-product-compliance
Lightning Source LLC
Chambersburg PA
CBHW080649180526
45168CB00008B/3355
* 9 7 8 1 5 1 7 4 8 9 9 8 4 *